'Inspiring children
to think big and dream big'

Dedicated to Daisy-Mae, Darcey and Eleanor -
The winners of ROAR2020

Daisy Mae, Darcey, and Eleanor were on a school trip to the recycling plant.

All three girls were passionate about saving the planet, even organizing school recycling drives every Earth Day, so they were excited to learn more about sustainability.

After departing the bus, the class was introduced to Anne, the woman in charge of the recycling plant. She would show everyone around and tell the class all about how the recycling plant worked.

"Let's start the tour!" Anne said.

The tour started in the plastics section. This was where all the plastic that people put into their recycling boxes came to be sorted, crushed, and given a new life.

Daisy-Mae noticed that the workers were discarding a lot of the plastic, throwing it into bins. It seemed like much of the plastic wasn't being recycled at all.

"Why aren't they recycling all the plastic?" Daisy-Mae asked, puzzled.

"Good question," Anne replied. She turned to the class to explain.

"The truth is, class, a huge amount of the plastic we recycle ends up in landfill.

When we receive your recycling here, there are a lot of plastic items that can't be given a new life."

"Is that because people don't clean or sort the items properly before they recycle them?" asked Darcey.

"No," said Anne. "It's because many items are made from plastic that can't be recycled, and companies want to keep it that way, because it's cheaper for them. Ordinary people want to recycle, but companies make it hard."

Anne continued.

"The word plastic covers a huge number of different materials, and all of them need to be recycled in different ways, if they can even be recycled at all. In one item of packaging, there could be several different plastics. At the recycling plant, the machines can only accept bundles of 100% pure plastic types. So even if there's one or two items in there that aren't PET plastic, for example, amid thousands of items, the bundle is useless and goes to landfill."

The class looked shocked.

As the tour through the recycling plant continued, the three young eco-warriors, Daisy-Mae, Darcey, and Eleanor, couldn't stop thinking about what they'd learned.

It was shocking that so much plastic and packaging still ended up in landfill, despite everyone doing their best to recycle.

The problem was made worse by greedy companies who continued to manufacture packaging that was so difficult to recycle. If only, the girls said, a solution could be found.

The bus journey back to school was long. While their classmates played games on their phones or chatted, Daisy-Mae, Darcey, and Eleanor hatched a plan.

They came up with an idea for an app that linked to a smart bin. The smart bin would scan a QR code on any packaging thrown into the bin, and information about the packaging's recyclability would appear on the linked app.

This would let people know exactly what their packaging was made of. It could be the start of real change.

"The app will let the consumer know how recyclable the packaging is," said Eleanor. "But there must be pressure on the companies too. How can we do that?"

"You're right," Darcey nodded. "The companies must change. Our app should drive that change."

"What if the app sent emails to the CEOs of the companies who make the packaging automatically, pressuring them to change their ways?" suggested Daisy-Mae.

"Wow, that's a great idea!" the girls agreed.

"So how would it work from start to finish?" wondered Eleanor.

The girls quickly produced a smooth process.

Download the app and connect the app via Bluetooth to your smart bin.

When you put rubbish in the bin, the bin scans the QR code on the packaging.

The app then displays information about the Environmental Damage Factor of the packaging, telling the consumer exactly what's made of.

The app uses graphs to break down exactly how much waste a household is producing in terms of Environmental Damage Factor.

If you can see the information laid out clearly, it's much easier to change your habits, produce less waste, and choose products that can be recycled easily. Companies will also be pressured by users of the app to produce more sustainable products, as each time an unsustainable product goes in the bin, the app will allow the user to send an email notifying the company that made it. It's a perfect process!

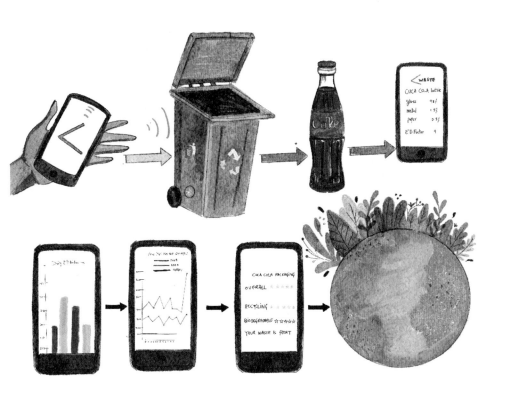

The girls all high-fived. "This is a great idea!"

"There's just one more thing. What will we name our app?"

"Well, it's an app that tackles waste," said Darcey. "Let's choose a simple name that tells people exactly what it does."

"How about Wasteless?" said Eleanor.

"Simple! I love it," said Daisy-Mae.

And so, Wasteless was born. With the app, the three eco-warriors were on a mission to change things for the better, use less packaging, and make a world to be proud of.

Have you got an idea,
like Daisy-Mae, Darcey and
Eleanor that could change
the world?

IDEA -

DRAW YOUR IDEA HERE -

8billBOOK
WASTELESS APP
ROAR2020

Printed in Great Britain
by Amazon